CW01460696

y

Text: *Carl Rogers*

Photographs: *Carl Rogers, Tony Bowerman, Fred Hughes, Porthmadog, mikeatkinson.net, © Crown copyright (2018) Visit Wales, Shutterstock*

Design: *Carl Rogers*

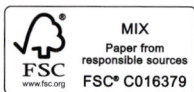

Ordnance Survey
Licensed Mapping

Partner

FSC
www.fsc.org

MIX
Paper from
responsible sources
FSC® C016379

Top 10 Walks series created by
Northern Eye Books

Cover: *Ynys Llanddwyn (walk 1)*
*Photo by Robert Stevens
@rob_stevens_photography*

Important Advice: The routes described in this book are undertaken at the reader's own risk. Walkers should take into account their level of fitness, wear suitable footwear and clothing, and carry food and water. It is also advisable to take the relevant OS map with you in case you get lost and leave the area covered by our maps.

Whilst every care has been taken to ensure the accuracy of the route directions, the publishers cannot accept responsibility for errors or omissions, or for changes in the details given. Nor can the publisher and copyright owners accept responsibility for any consequences arising from the use of this book.

If you find any inaccuracies in either the text or maps, please write or email us at the address below. Thank you.

First published in 2018.
Second Ed published in 2020, reprinted 2021 by: :

MARA BOOKS

*22 Crosland Terrace, Helsby,
Cheshire WA6 9LY*

e-mail: carl@marabooks.co.uk
tel: 01928 723 744

Twitter   @WalesCoastUK
                     @CarlMaraBooks

Instagram   @wales_coast_path
                     @carlrogers1960

www.walescoastpath.co.uk
www.northerneyebooks.co.uk

Printed & bound in the UK by Charlesworth Press

Contents

The **Wales Coast Path**

WALES IS THE ONLY COUNTRY IN THE WORLD with a path around its entire coast. The long-distance **Wales Coast Path** offers 870 miles/1400 kilometres of unbroken coastal walking, from the outskirts of the walled city of Chester in the north to the market town of Chepstow in the south.

There's something new around every corner. Visually stunning and rich in both history and wildlife, the path promises ever-changing views, wildflowers and seabirds, as well as castles, coves and coastal pubs. In fact, the Wales Coast Path runs through 1 Marine Nature Reserve, 2 National Parks, 3 Areas of Outstanding Natural Beauty, 11 National Nature Reserves, 14 Heritage Coasts, and 23 Historic Landscapes. And, to cap it all, the **Wales Coast Path** links up with the long-distance Offa's Dyke Path at either end: creating a complete, 1,030 mile circuit of the whole of Wales.

Aberffraw

Isle of **Anglesey**/Ynys Môn

The **Isle of Anglesey** (Ynys Môn) is Wales' largest island and boasts a varied coastline of over 130 miles (210 kilometres) with some of the grandest coastal scenery in the whole of Wales. The **Isle of Anglesey Coastal Path** and the **Wales Coast Path** both circle the island giving access to one of the most varied sections of coast in Wales.

Sea cliffs, offshore rocks and tiny coves dominate the northern and western coasts, while the island's gentler eastern side promises sandy beaches backed by woods and resorts like Benllech and Moelfre. The southern shore is a complete contrast bordering the river-like Menai Strait.

> "The sleepy sound of a tea-time tide
> Slaps at the rocks the sun has dried,
> Too lazy, almost, to sink and lift
> Round low peninsulas pink with thrift"

A Bay In Anglesey, John Betjeman

TOP 10 Walks: Isle of Anglesey/Ynys Môn

THE ISLE OF ANGLESEY offers some of the finest coastal walking in North Wales. In a circuit of around 130 miles, there are dramatic sea cliffs, quiet coves, wide sandy bays, tiny fishing villages, modern resorts, coastal hills and remains from a rich maritime heritage. The walks in this book are what I consider to be the finest routes along this superb section of coast, one of the seven main sections of the **Wales Coast Path**.

Ynys Llanddwyn — page 8

Aberffraw — page 14

Rhoscolyn — page 20

South Stack — page 26

Carmel Head
page 32

Cemlyn Bay
page 38

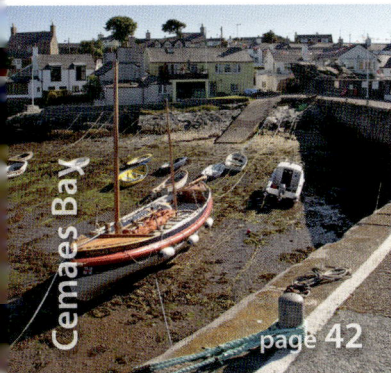

Cemaes Bay
page 42

Point Lynas
page 48

Traeth Lligwy
page 54

Moelfre
page 58

Twr Mawr lighthouse on Llanddwyn Island and the distant hills of Llŷn

Ynys Llanddwyn

A walk along one of the finest beaches in Wales. Sandy paths, forest trails and some beach walking

Distance/time: 9.5 kilometres / 6 miles. Allow 2½ hours

Start: Forestry Commission car park in Newborough Forest. Fee payable on entry to the forest

Grid ref: SH 405 633

Ordnance Survey Map: Explorer 263 Anglesey East: *Beaumaris, Amlwch & Menai Bridge*

After the walk: Picnic area at the car park. Pub and café in nearby Newborough and Malltraeth

What to expect:

Sandy paths, soft in places, beach walking and forest tracks

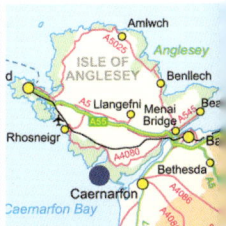

Walk outline

From the forest car park the route heads out across the beach to Ynys Llanddwyn, one of the most dramatic island locations in Wales. After a circuit of the island and a section of beach, the route heads into the conifer plantations of Newborough Forest. Some rough sandy tracks will be encountered on the edge of the forest.

Ynys Llanddwyn

Ynys Llanddwyn is named after the Celtic Saint Dwynwen, who is said to have retreated to this remote corner of Wales after a failed love match with an infatuated Welsh prince. The shrine she established attracted love sick pilgrims throughout the Middle Ages. Today, visitors are more likely to be attracted by the stunning views and spectacular location.

Backed by the plantations of Newborough Forest, with the extensive Cefni estuary to the north and the nearby sand dunes of Newborough Warren, this is one of the most unique locations in Wales. Keep and eye out for grey seals around Ynys Llanddwyn and the growing population of our native red squirrels in Newborough Forest.

Ancient shipwreck

Red squirrel

The Walk

1. From the **Forest car park** take the **beach access path** in the bottom corner and turn right along the sand towards Ynys Llanddwyn.

At low tide the sandy bay curves out to the island and it is a straightforward walk across the sand to reach it. (**Note:** During the highest tides you may have to use the remains of an ancient stone causeway to reach the island or even wait for the tide to turn.)

2. There is an obvious **large information sign/shelter** as you reach the island. The broad track/path ahead leads directly to the southern tip of **Ynys Llanddwyn**, but a path on the left takes you on a more interesting route around the southeastern side of the island. Access this path through the **carved**

Please note: Dogs are not allowed on the island from May 1 – Sep 30.

Newborough Forest is one of the UK's rare coastal woodlands

wooden gate on the left, behind the information sign. The path is surfaced with crushed shells and leads above the sandy cove of **Porth y Cwch** with its grand view out to Snowdonia. Continue until you reach a junction of paths by a **stone cross** with the remains of **Eglwyseg Dwynwen** opposite.

Turn left here towards the lighthouse passing the **Pilots' Cottages**. The path swings round to a path junction directly below the main lighthouse.

The Pilots' Cottages once housed the Llanddwyn shipping pilots and their
families. The small cannon that stands in front of the cottages was used throughout this period to summon the lifeboat and crew in times of distress.

3. Turn left up steps to visit the lighthouse or right up towards another **stone cross**. Pass the cross and continue on the good path around the northwest edge of the island. At a T-junction with a broad path, turn left through the **carved gate** and follow the broad path back to the information sign passed earlier.

Leaving the island bear left onto **Traeth Penrhos**, the vast expanse of sand to

Ynys Llanddwyn is one of the most spectacular locations in Wales

the north of Ynys Llanddwyn. Within the first 200 metres or so look for a gap in the sand dunes and bear right through the dunes.

Recent erosion has partly buried an old forest path that runs behind the dunes. When you locate this path turn left and walk behind the dunes parallel to the beach with the forest over to the right.

The path emerges from the wind-blown sand and becomes better defined as you continue, with the dead and dying remains of the forest on either side.

4. The path eventually enters the woods again and in around 1 kilometre/¾ mile

or so, there is a **sharp right-hand bend** where you join the **Wales Coast Path**. Turn right and stay on this broad forest road for about 1.5 kilometres/1 mile.

Newborough Forest was planted in the 1950s to stabilise a vast area of moving sand dunes formed over the last 700 years by prevailing southwesterly winds. Today, it is a working forest producing over 10,000 tonnes of timber per year and has been designated as a Site of Special Scientific Interest.

5. Turn right at a T-junction (**post number 9**). This track descends to pass **post 6**, then curves left and begins to rise. Turn right at **post number 5** onto a forest path. This emerges at a small **car park** by the beach. Turn left and follow the road out of the car park and through the woods, returning to the large **Newborough Forest car park** to complete the walk. ♦

Lovers' island?

Llanddwyn Island is named after Saint Dwynwen, who retreated to this remote location after a failed love match with a young prince. The prince was so infatuated with her that he could not wait for their marriage and tried to seduce her. The resistance she made resulted in rejection. Dwynwen vowed to become a nun and retreated to this remote corner of Anglesey to be alone. The shrine that she established here attracted love sick pilgrims throughout the Middle Ages.

Morning light on the stunning beach at Aberffraw

Aberffraw

Easy walking along a section of gentle coast with superb views across Caernarfon Bay to the hills of Llŷn

Distance/time: 10 kilometres / 6¼ miles. Allow 3 hours

Start: There is free parking available for a number of cars on common land beside the old bridge at Aberffraw.

Grid ref: SH 356 689

Ordnance Survey Map: Explorer 262 Anglesey West: *Holyhead/ Caergybi*

After the walk: 'Y Goron' ('The Crown'), in Aberffraw, or 'The Oystercatcher' at nearby Rhosneigr.

What to expect:
Straightforward coastal path, sand dunes and quiet lane

Walk outline

A walk of two contrasting loops — the first loop weaves through the extensive sand dunes to the east of the village with a return along the beach. The second loop explores the gentle coast with a visit to one of the most remarkable churches in Wales: the tiny church of St Cwyfan in the rocky cove of Porth Cwyfan. The return to Aberffraw is along a quiet lane.

Aberffraw

The tiny village of Aberffraw was once the political centre of the ancient kingdom of Gwynedd, but there is not the slightest hint of it today. The site of the royal palace is lost and the sea port that existed here lies buried beneath the extensive sands that clog Afon Ffraw. And thankfully so, Aberffraw has one of the most spectacular beaches on the island and the gentle coast explored on this walk is quiet and unspoilt.

In summer the low, grassy cliffs are pink with thrift and pyramidal orchids; this is a good place to see grey seals, too, hauled out on the rocks or idling in the shallow clear water. You can also enjoy stunning views across the bay to the hills of Llŷn.

The old bridge, Aberffraw

Thrift or 'sea pinks'

The Walk

1. From the **old bridge** turn left (away from the village) and take the **lane** (right fork) that heads off across the **common**. Pass the **signed Coast Path** on the right and in another 80 metres or so, bear right taking one of the footpaths that cut across the grassy dunes.

The exact line you take is not critical as this is open access land and there are many faint paths to choose from. The most obvious path takes a line parallel to the lane at first, then gradually veers away right-wards.

The common is open and flat initially before the grassy backs of the dunes begin to rise on the right. Keep these grassy dunes on your right and continue ahead until there are **fenced fields** ahead. You should meet a **well-used beach path** here. Turn right and follow this down to the **beach**.

This is one of the most beautiful bays in Wales and is perhaps seen at its best on a clear summer evening when the crowds have left. Across the shallow clear waters of Caernarfon Bay, the blue outlines of Gryn Ddu, Yr Eifl and the hills of the Llŷn Peninsula line the horizon, while the higher peaks of Snowdonia peep over the headland at the end of the bay.

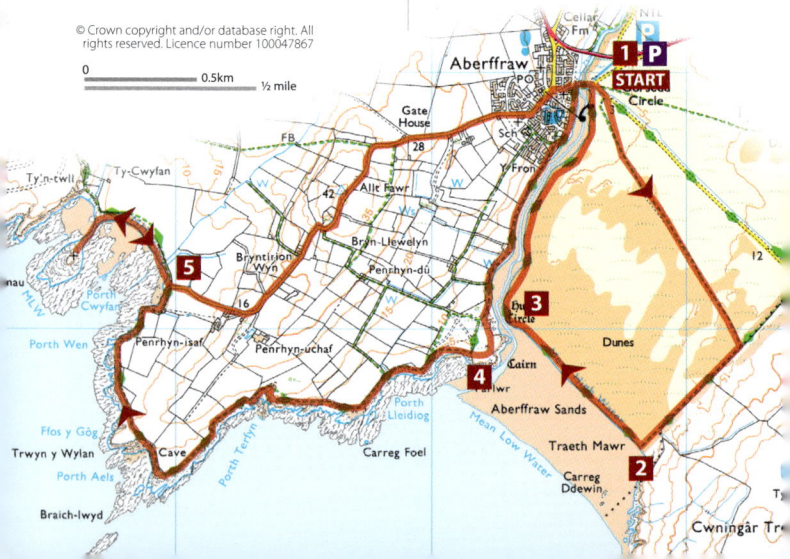

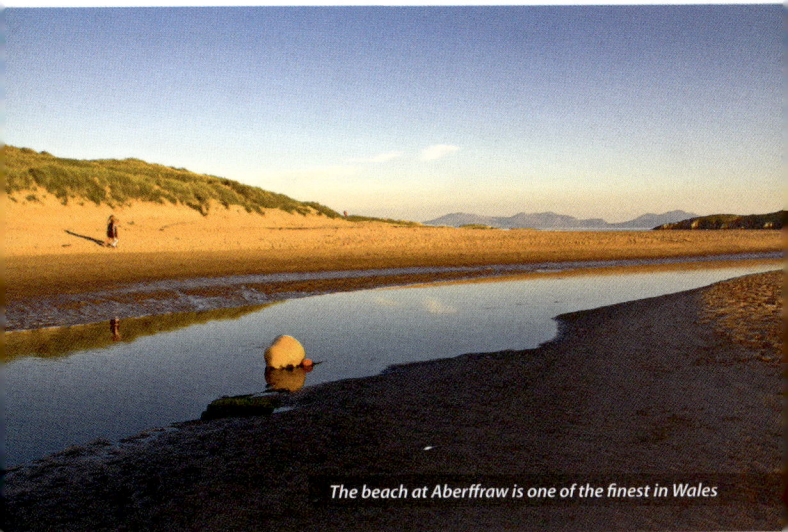

The beach at Aberffraw is one of the finest in Wales

2. Turn right along the sand. The beach is around half-a-mile long, the far end being the mouth of **Afon Ffraw** giving the village its name.

3. When you reach the river turn right and follow the river bank back to the old bridge by the car park. First loop complete!

To continue the walk, cross the **old stone bridge** and turn left immediately onto an unmade **tidal road** that follows the river bank. Where the road bears left onto the sand, continue along the shore to the mouth of the river. The signed coast path to the right here can be used if the tide is high.

Originally, Aberffraw was open to the sea and even enjoyed a brief period of prosperity as a small port. Over the centuries however, the estuary has become filled with sand and today over half a mile of sand dunes separate it from the sea.

Surprisingly, there is nothing at Aberffraw to suggest its past importance as the administrative centre for the kingdom of Gwynedd. For eight hundred years, Welsh kings and princes used the royal palace at Aberffraw as a base in their fight against

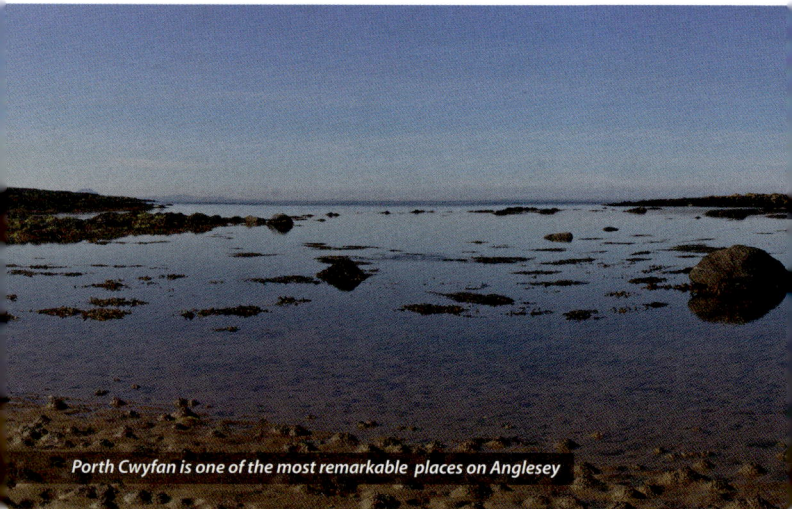

Porth Cwyfan is one of the most remarkable places on Anglesey

invasions from Irish, Saxons, Vikings and finally Normans.

The reason for the absence of remains is the exclusive use of wood. The building of castles and churches from stone did not really begin until after the Norman conquest and even then, the earliest motte and bailey castles were usually of timber construction. Strange as this may seem today, Anglesey was thickly wooded until the Middle Ages, so timber would have been plentiful. In 1317 however, the palace at Aberffraw was demolished and its timbers used to repair Caernarfon Castle.

4. Near the mouth of the river, bear right through a **kissing gate** and swing right over the open headland.

The coastal path from here is easy to follow and keeps to the edge of the low rocks with occasional departures into **small coves** and onto wave-cut rocks.

At the first cove, steps lead down onto the shingle. This is followed by a short section over the flat rocks ahead before the path becomes clear again. Ignore a path to the right. Keep your eyes open for grey seals on this section.

Continue to **Porth Cwyfan**, a wide, rocky bay with a tiny **church on a small island**. At low tide it is just a short

walk along the beach where a ruined causeway takes you onto the island.

5. Return to the lane access and turn left. Follow the lane back to Aberffraw (just over 1.75 kilometres/1 mile).

As you enter the village turn right by the post office. Pass **Y Goron** ('The Crown') pub and continue down to cross the **old bridge** to complete the walk. ♦

St Cwyfan's Church

Saint Cwyfan's is a tiny Celtic church in a remarkable setting. Founded in the seventh century, it was rebuilt in stone during the twelfth century and fully restored in the nineteenth century. Despite this, it has managed to retain its original simple form. The stone wall which surrounds the island was built during the nineteenth century restoration to counteract severe erosion problems.

Kayaks at Porth y Corwgl

Rhoscolyn 🐦

A fine, rugged section of the Coast Path around the
southern tip of Holy Island with wide views to Snowdonia

Distance/time: 8.5 kilometres / 5¼ miles. Allow 3 hours

Start: A few cars can be parked beside Saint Gwenfaen's Church, Rhoscolyn

Grid ref: SH 269 758

Ordnance Survey Map: Explorer 262 Anglesey West: *Holyhead/Caergybi*

After the walk: The 'White Eagle' pub, Rhoscolyn | 01407 860267 | www.white-eagle.co.uk

What to expect:

Good coastal path, narrow in places. Farmland paths sometimes with cattle

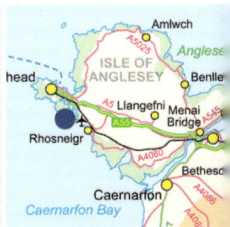

Walk outline

Quiet lanes and farmland paths lead down to the picturesque sands of Silver Bay where the Anglesey Coast Path is joined. The coast path is then followed across open coastal heath to Borthwen at Rhoscolyn before a section of rugged coast, with the option of a short detour to the natural sea arch of Bwa Gwyn. The return is by easy farmland path.

Rhoscolyn

Rhoscolyn is a well known centre for sailing and watersports, but also has some of the finest coastal scenery on Anglesey, backed by spectacular views of Snowdonia and the shapely hills of the Llŷn Peninsula. Of note are the dramatic sea cliffs around Rhoscolyn Head and the fine sandy beaches at Silver Bay and Borthwen.

The pockets of coastal heath around Silver Bay and Rhoscolyn Head, provide a unique habitat bright with heather and maritime wildflowers. The cliffs also give good vantage points for viewing passing porpoise and bottlenoise dolphins. Watch, too, for impressively large, black and white gannets who can occasionally be seen offshore diving for shoals of mackerel.

Silver Bay

Gannet

The sweeping panorama from Rhoscolyn Coastguard Lookout

The Walk

1. With the **church** behind you, bear right along the lane. Ignore the first right (this leads down to the beach), instead, keep ahead along the lane and take the next right, signed to 'Silver Bay'.

Follow the lane for 400 metres and on a sharp **right-hand bend** bear left along an access road (marked as a dead end). Ignore the signed Coast Path on the left in around 100 metres or so, continuing along the lane to the house **Bryn y Bar**.

2. Cross a **stile** to the left of the house and head across the following field just

to the right of centre, towards **pine woods**. Go through a kissing gate and along a **board walk** to pass through a small pine wood. Emerge onto the fine, **sandy beach** at **Silver Bay**.

Turn right along the sand. Just past the **beach access road**, turn right up a **concrete ramp**, signed for the Coast Path. At the access road, take the signed Coast Path on the left. Keep left of a **flag pole** and a little further on the coast path swings right along the edge of **open coastal heath**.

After a kissing gate, go ahead across a

small field backing the tiny rocky cove of **Porth Gorsiwyn**. After another kissing gate, the path continues along more open, coastal heath, eventually reaching a gate by **houses**. Go through the gate and bear right along an access track. At a T-junction turn left and at the gate to **Cil Bwch** turn right onto a footpath. At a junction ignore a footpath on the right, continuing ahead along the path between gardens and the beach (over to the left) to reach a **lane**.

3. Turn left down the lane passing through the **beach car park** and onto the **beach**. Go right along the sand, or, if the tide is high, follow the path along the top of a **concrete wall** that backs the beach and drop down onto

the sand at the end. About 200 metres further on, bear right up a **slipway** to follow an access road between houses passing a small cove — **Porth y Corwgl** — on the left. Just before 'The Point' bear right up a driveway and take the signed path to the right of the driveway to 'Bryn Eithin'. Immediately after a **cottage** on the left, turn left on the signed path between **gardens**. Stay with this path eventually passing another **house** on the right.

Cross the access road to **The Point** and go through the kissing gate opposite into **grazing fields**. Rise through the fields now, aiming for the **coastguard lookout** on the skyline.

It is worth a short detour to see the natural sea arch of Bwa Gwyn

From the lookout in clear weather there is a grand view over much of Caernarfon Bay. To the north, Holyhead Mountain, with the lighthouse flashing at South Stack, can be seen in the distance, along with the chimney of the aluminium works near Holyhead. Southwards lie the sandy coves and islets around Rhoscolyn, with Rhosneigr and the headland at Aberffraw across the channel on Anglesey.

4. From the lookout, continue on the grassy path through grazing fields to **Ffynnon Gwenfaen** (see box opposite). This lies near the edge of the cliffs about 600 metres away.

Beyond the well, pass through a kissing gate on the **edge of the cliffs** and follow the path along the top of a large crag overhanging the sea (take care here). The path stays close to the **wall** on the right, which soon turns right.

At the next inlet (**Porth Saint**) there is a little **footbridge** and a footpath down to the rocky cove.

(It is worth a short detour here to see Bwa Gwyn — a natural sea arch. For this, continue along the coastal footpath through a kissing gate and along the large crags for about 300 metres. The arch is down to the left. Return to the little footbridge to continue).

5. Immediately after the footbridge, bear right through a kissing gate and walk ahead between **old field boundary walls** and towards a large **farmhouse**. The path keeps to the left of the farm and farmyard to join the access lane.

Turn left and follow the lane back to **Saint Gwenfaen's Church** to complete the walk. ♦

Holy Well

The small stone enclosure on the clifftop near Rhoscolyn Head is Saint Gwenfaen's Well; the remains of a medieval healing well. It has stone steps, corner seats and may have originally been roofed. During the Middle Ages, like so many other sites, it became a place of pilgrimage — a gift of two white quartz pebbles thrown into the pool were believed to cure mental health problems.

South Stack Lighthouse

South Stack

A walk visiting the highest sea cliffs on Anglesey along with one of the most iconic lighthouses in Wales

What to expect:
Open heath, coastal path with some big drops into the sea in places

Distance/time: 8 kilometres / 5 miles (add 0.5 kilometres / ¼ mile and 15 mins for summit detour). Allow 2½ to 3½ hours

Start: Car park, RSPB South Stack Visitor Centre

Grid ref: SH 208 821

Ordnance Survey Map: Explorer 262 Anglesey West: *Holyhead/ Caergybi*

After the walk: RSPB South Stack Cliffs Visitor Centre Café | 01407 762100 | www.rspb.org.uk

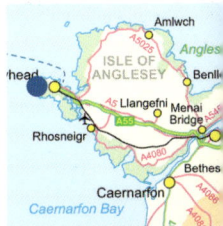

Walk outline

Starting at the RSPB Visitor Centre, this walk takes you over the low southern shoulder of Holyhead Mountain to the Breakwater Coastal Park. The Coast Path is then followed to North Stack, before climbing towards Holyhead Mountain with the option to take in the highest summit on Anglesey. The walk finishes with a visit to the iconic South Stack Lighthouse and the RSPB viewing centre at Ellin's Tower.

South Stack and Holyhead Mountain

South Stack, with its iconic lighthouse and dramatic cliff scenery, is one of the most famous locations in Wales. The sea cliffs here are the highest on the island exceeding 500 feet around Gogarth Bay, whilst the nearby summit of Holyhead Mountain is the highest point on Anglesey, offering views across the island to Snowdonia and out over the Irish Sea to Ireland in clear weather.

Bird watchers will be interested in the RSPB information centre at Ellin's Tower where seabirds can be viewed through video links. During the summer months, you can thrill to the thousands of noisy breeding seabirds crammed onto the cliff ledges: guillemots, razorbills and fulmars.

Folded rocks, South Stack

Breeding fulmars

Ellin's Tower — RSPB information and viewing centre

The Walk

1. From the **RSPB car park** entrance take the signed footpath opposite and a little to the right. The right of way follows a tarmac track through a small field, then, after a second gate, a tarmac footpath across open moorland.

2. At the junction of paths near a **fenced stone building**, bear right onto a broad gravel path. Stay on this path heading towards the craggy face of Holyhead Mountain. As you approach the crags, the path narrows and swings right, making a gentle rise (yellow markers). Keep ahead now ignoring paths on either side, passing a **row of cottages** over to the right and small walled fields with young pines also on the right.

3. Keep ahead at a **junction of paths between stone walls**. *Soon the harbour and breakwater come into view.* Continue ahead between **stone walls** soon with **allotments** on your right.

4. At an access drive with a house ahead, bear left along a grassy path to reach a **lane**. Turn left along the lane and in around 50 metres go

straight ahead at a fork passing close to **a house** on your right, then steeply down a **series of steps** with **Holyhead Breakwater Country Park** beneath you on the left.

5. At the bottom of the steps bear left to reach the **entrance to the country park** on your left. Go ahead over the road and follow the footpath beside the **lake**. Beyond the lake, take the signed foot path in the corner on the right. Turn left immediately along a track and in 50 metres or so, bear right through a carved wooden gate on the signed Coast Path. The path goes ahead through rough grass towards the large **quarry face** ahead.

6. As you approach the cliff face the path curves right to a point overlooking the sea with a wide view back to Holyhead harbour. The path swings left here up **stone steps** to contour the open hillside high above the sea. Stay on the pitched path ignoring minor paths here and there and soon you will be able to see along the coast to the buildings at **North Stack**. After the little

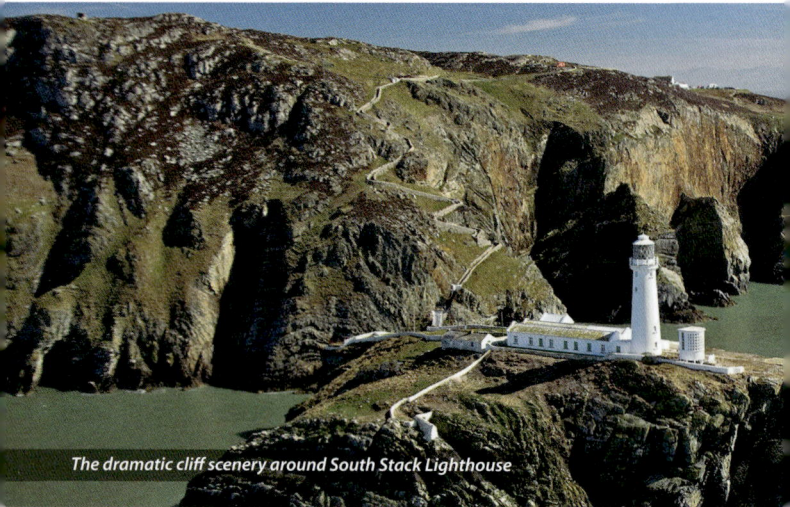

The dramatic cliff scenery around South Stack Lighthouse

magazine building the path begins a steady rise to a T-junction. Turn right.

Where the path forks, bear right down to the buildings at North Stack.

North Stack is the site of a redundant fog warning station, which includes the Trinity House Magazine, built in 1861, where shells for the warning cannon were stored.

7. To continue, walk back up the track. Where it begins to level the Coast Path bears right off the track and begins the steady climb, in a series of steps, up towards **Holyhead Mountain**.

The path levels as you pass through **stone walls** then makes a slight drop to a broad saddle. Take the right fork here, rising again up onto the shoulder of the mountain.

(To include the summit of Holyhead Mountain, take the signed path at the top of the rise on the left. Return to this point to continue.)

8. The path continues ahead, soon much broader with a good gravel surface. Ignore paths on either side and after passing the **fenced modern stone building** seen earlier in the walk, cross the access road. Follow the stony footpath opposite passing close to **brick buildings** on the left beneath a **radio mast**.

This path passes a **small pool** down to the left. Soon you will find yourself in a dramatic position overlooking **South Stack Lighthouse**. Head half-left from here to reach a road end directly above the lighthouse.

Turn left along the road. Shortly take the signed coast path down to **Ellin's Tower** information centre. Pass the tower and follow the cliff top path back to the car park to complete the walk. ♦

Ellin's Tower

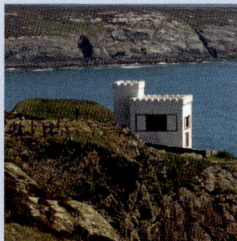

Ellin's Tower was built as a summer retreat for Ellin, the wife of William Stanley in 1867. She was a keen observer of the bird life to be found around South Stack. After Ellin's death the tower became a popular attraction in the closing years of the nineteenth century, before falling into decay after World War II. In 1980 it was bought by the RSPB who carried out renovation work and opened it to the public as an information centre and bird hide in 1982.

Carmel Head and one of the curious White Ladies

Carmel Head

A spectacular walk around the remote northwest tip of Anglesey with wide views

What to ex...
*Coastal path cl...
cliff edges in place...
Some stretches along...
quiet lanes/farm tracks*

Distance/time: 8 kilometres / 5 miles. Allow 2-3 hours

Start: Small car park situated on a bend in the narrow land heading south from Mynachdy farm. This can be reached by taking the lane west from the village of Llanfairynghornwy

Grid ref: SH 303 914

Ordnance Survey Map: Explorer 262 Anglesey West: *Holyhead/Caergybi*

After the walk: Pubs and cafés in Cemaes Bay

Walk outline

A path across farmland leads down to the hidden rocky cove and unusual pool by the islet of Ynys y Fydlyn. The Coast Path is joined here and followed north to Carmel Head — high sea cliffs and wide views out to Holy Island and The Skerries can be enjoyed along this section. Beyond Carmel Head the coast is lower and more gentle but there are impressive tide races as the sea moves over rocks close to the surface. From Hen Borth farm tracks and quiet lanes are used to return to the car park.

The White Ladies markers

Carmel Head

This section of the coast is one of the quietest and least visited on the island. After the dramatic cliff scenery around Ynys y Fydlyn, the north coast is surprisingly gentle and low lying and feels more like the Hebrides than Wales. Access is by narrow lanes and there are no villages or resorts on the coast. Carmel Head is famous for the impressive tide race which reverses direction with each tide.

Keep a lookout for Atlantic grey seals, which can often be seen basking on the rocks, porpoise and bottlenose dolphins.

Atlantic grey seal

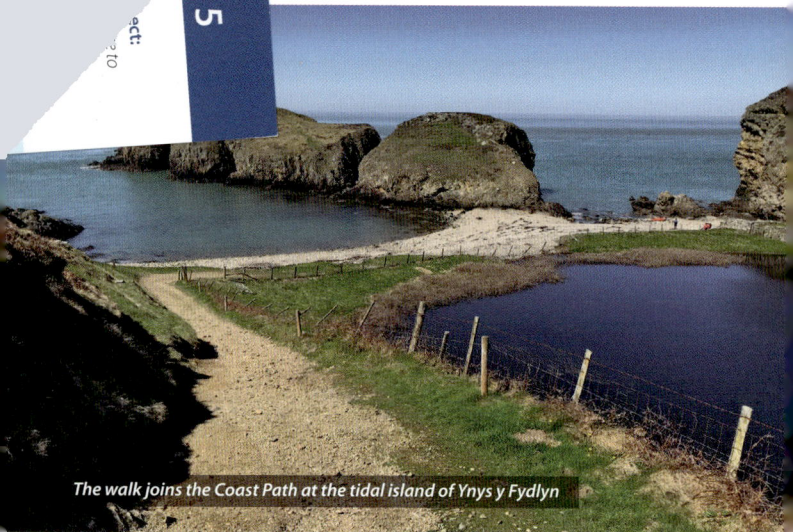

The walk joins the Coast Path at the tidal island of Ynys y Fydlyn

The Walk

1. Follow the **farm track** out of the car park. In a 150 metres or so, and just before a crossing track, the right of way veers left off the track and soon crosses two stiles. With little visible on the ground, the right of way keeps ahead aiming more or less for a **square brick tower** visible ahead. Further on, **woods** appear over to the right and soon you are looking down to the attractive, rocky cove and tidal island of **Ynys y Fydlyn**.

2. Follow the path down to the cove and turn right along the shingle beach.

At the far end, go through the kissing gate and take the path that zig-zags up onto high sea cliffs above Ynys y Fydlyn. The path is narrow and close to the cliff edge in places so care is needed. Pass through an area of **stunted pines** and rough ground above the cliff-lined cove of **Porth yr Hwch** to reach the more gentle open grassland of **Penbryneglwys**, the western extremity of **Carmel Head**. A **small rocky summit** high above the sea makes a good picnic spot in calm weather.

The view takes in the wide sweep of

Holyhead Bay to the port of Holyhead on Holy Island and out to the group of rocks known as The Skerries. Originally, The Skerries were owned by Bangor Cathedral but were diverted into private ownership by Bishop Nicholas Robinson during the 1570s. In 1713, the islands were leased by a descendant of the Bishop's to William Tench. He built the first beacon here in 1716 and planned to collect duties from shipping entering Holyhead, however, the venture proved to be disastrous and he died penniless in 1725. Tragically, he also lost his son, who drowned while ferrying coal to The Skerries to keep the beacon running. Another tragedy happened to a descendant of Bishop Robinson in June 1739, when William Robinson and twelve companions drowned while returning from the beacon. Their empty boat was washed ashore four days later in Cumbria.

3. There is little sign of a path on the ground here, so aim for the distant **tower** visible on the islet of **West Mouse**. Soon the angular bulk of **Wylfa Power Station** comes into view and a little further on a **chimney** associated with mines nearby. The coast path passes directly below the chimney on the left-hand side.

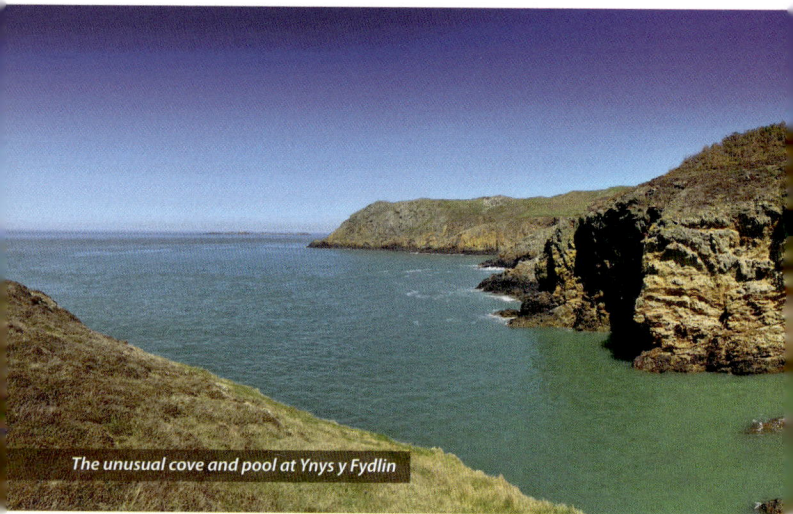

The unusual cove and pool at Ynys y Fydlin

The two pyramidal towers that can be seen close to the chimney are known as the 'White Ladies'. These line up with a similar tower on West Mouse and acted as a guide for shipping negotiating Carmel Head.

From the chimney, head towards the left-hand tower (the one closest to the coast). Cross a **wooden footbridge**, pass to the left of the tower and head for a kissing gate in the wall ahead.

4. The coast path is now straightforward and passes along the edge of grazing fields and low cliffs for around 1.5kilometres/1 mile.

5. Beyond the National Trust Land at Tyn

Llan you reach the broad shingle bay of **Hen Borth** and the path follows the low cliffs as they curve right into the bay.

Immediately before a small **farm bridge** over a **stream**, turn right through a kissing gate. Cross a field and go through a second kissing gate. The path keeps beside the stream to reach a lane.

Turn right immediately over a stile beside the gate to 'Hen Felin'. Follow a grass farm track past the **cottage** and into a large field. Follow the right of way directly ahead beneath **overhead power cables**.

The path soon becomes a farm track.

Follow this to the large farm ahead (**Mynachdy**).

Entering the farmyard, turn left beside the farmhouse and follow the access road away from the farm. At the lane bear right (ahead) and follow the lane back to the little car park to complete the walk. ♦

The Skerries

Northwest of Carmel Head lies the group of rocks known as The Skerries — a Norse name and one of the surprisingly few legacies from the Norse raids of over 1,000 years ago. It is derived from the word 'sker' meaning 'steep rock'. In Welsh they are known as Ynysoedd y Moelrhoniaid or 'Seal Islands'. The Skerries became the last privately owned lighthouse in the country and was eventually sold for the record sum of £440,984 in 1844.

The unusual beach and lagoon at Cemlyn Bay

Cemlyn Bay 🐦

A short, fascinating walk in a quiet, remote corner of the island visiting one of the largest tern colonies in the UK

What to expect:

Awkward walking on the shingle beach followed by grassy coastal path

Distance/time: 5.5 kilometres / 3½ miles. Allow 2 hours

Start: Free car park at the eastern end of Cemlyn Bay. This is approached via a narrow lane, which leaves the A5025 at Tregele. Alternative parking to avoid the beach section SH 329 936

Grid ref: SH 336 932

Ordnance Survey Map: Explorer 262 Anglesey West: *Holyhead/Caergybi*

After the walk: Pubs and cafés in Cemaes Bay 3 miles east.

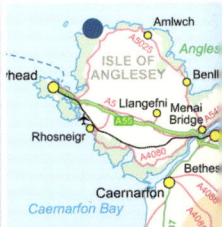

Walk outline

The walk begins with the unusual Esgair Cemlyn — a ridge of shingle deposited by winter storms that contains the Cemlyn Lagoon and the site of the Cemlyn tern colony. This is followed by easy coast path around the grassy head of Trwyn Cemlyn and along the coast to Hen Borth. The return loop takes you past the tiny medieval church of Saint Rhwydrus.

Cemlyn Bay

Cemlyn Bay is famous for its unusual shingle beach — formed by storm waves depositing shingle across the mouth of the bay. This contains a tidal lagoon which supports one of the largest tern colonies in the UK. Access along the beach is restricted between April and August to protect the colony when the birds are nesting.

Also of note is the large walled nature reserve and house of Bryn Aber, once home of Captain Vivian Hewitt, the first person to fly across the Irish Sea. He moved here in the 1930s and created a wildlife sanctuary. The high wall protected trees and bushes which attracted migratory birds. He also built the dam that maintains the water level in the lagoon.

Lifeboat memorial

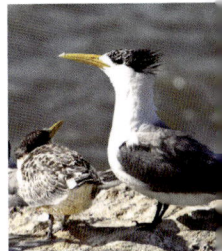
Sandwich tern

The Walk

1. From the car park , take the path along the top of the shingle ridge above the beach. **NB** *between 1 April and 31 August this path will be closed when the terns are nesting and you will need to walk along the shingle beach. Markers will make the detour clear*.

At the far end of the beach, cross the **concrete footbridge** to reach the road and second car park (alternative start). Turn right along the rough road and follow it past the **lifeboat monument** and out onto the open grassy headland of **Trwyn Cemlyn**. A grass path circles the headland.

The memorial commemorates the 150th anniversary of the first lifeboat on Anglesey (1828-1978). This was founded by the Reverend James Williams and his wife Frances after witnessing the wreck of the Irish Packet 'Alert' which drifted onto West Mouse killing 145 people in 1823.

2. The path eventually leads to a kissing gate in a wall corner. Go through the gate and follow the coast path along the field edge overlooking the sea.

The way is clear for almost a mile to **Hen Borth**, a broad rocky bay.

As the path drops gently to Hen Borth, you will see a tiny church isolated in the fields down to your left.

3. Descend the field and as the slope levels, don't go through the kissing gate ahead, instead turn sharp left and aim directly for the little church. A gate and steps to the left of the church lead into the cemetery.

*This is the tiny, ancient **church of Saint Rhwydrus**, one of the most isolated medieval churches on Anglesey. It was founded in the sixth century, and sections of the current building date from the twelfth. In the little cemetery there are graves dating back to 1675 as well as the*

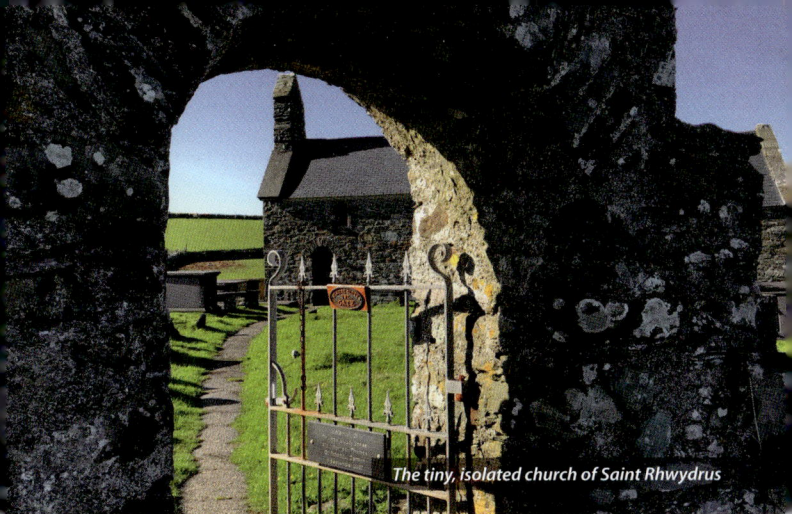
The tiny, isolated church of Saint Rhwydrus

grave of Christen Osuldsen, a Norwegian sea captain, presumably shipwrecked nearby.

Leave the church cemetery by the same gate and turn right towards a **farm**. Pass through the farmyard and keep ahead down the access road.

At the T-junction turn left and follow the road beside the lagoon and the high brick walls of **Bryn Aber**, *once the home of Captain Vivian Hewitt, the first man to fly across the Irish Sea. The high wall was built as a bird sanctuary.*

Turn right across the concrete footbridge and return along the beach to compete the walk.♦

Tern Colony
Cemlyn beach is the breeding site of one of the largest tern colonies in Britain and birds return here each spring. The reserve provides a unique opportunity to view a tern colony at such close quarters, although you are requested to follow the viewing instructions so as not to disturb birds during the breeding season. Please do not walk along the ridge between April and August when the birds are nesting.

Cemaes Bay

Cemaes Bay

An impressive walk along a section of remote and rugged coast with high sea cliffs and wide views

What to expect:
Good coastal path, narrow in places with some high sea cliffs and wide views

Distance/time: 9 kilometres / 5½ miles. Allow 2-3 hours

Start: There is a small car park with toilet facilities near the harbour in the village of Cemaes Bay

Grid ref: SH 373 935

Ordnance Survey Map: Explorer 262 Anglesey West: *Holyhead/ Caergybi*

After the walk: Pubs, and cafés in Cemaes Bay

Walk outline

Starting in the village of Cemaes Bay, the route heads east along the bay to the little church of Llanbadrig perched on the edge of the sea cliffs. The coast path is then followed eastwards to the wide rocky inlet of Porth Wen. This is an impressive section of coast with high sea cliffs and one or two rocky coves. The return leg is along a quiet lane and finally field paths.

Cemaes Bay

Cemaes originated as a tiny, remote fishing settlement at a time when poor roads made travel by sea the only reliable link with the outside world. This led to the development of the small harbour allowing ships from Cemaes to trade in coal, limestone, corn, marble, lime and ochre. An indication of Cemaes' commercial links with England can be seen by the fact that many public buildings in Liverpool are built from limestone and marble exported from Cemaes.

Today the village markets itself as a holiday resort. There is a fine, safe beach and the surrounding coastal scenery is amongst the finest on the island. It is also a popular location for fishing, sailing and birdwatching.

Ruins at Llanlleiana

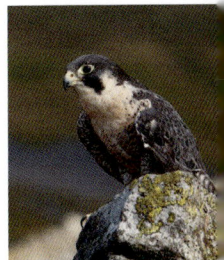
Peregrine

The Walk

1. From the **car park**, head eastwards (away from the village) along the sea front to a **second car park** at the end of a narrow lane. The signed coast path leaves the lane on the left at the car park entrance (**National Trust land, Penrhyn Mawr**). Turn left onto this path and follow it up onto the low cliffs overlooking the bay.

The coast path weaves along field edges to **Porth Padrig**, Cemaes' most easterly beach and too far from local facilities to be overcrowded. At the beach access you can make a short detour left onto the sand or bear right to where a kissing gate leads into a quiet **lane**. Turn left

now and follow the lane to the tiny church of **Llanbadrig**.

Dedicated to Saint Patrick, the present building is a small structure, just 60 feet by 14 feet and stands on the very edge of the cliffs, defying the frequent winter gales which sweep in from the Irish Sea. It is mainly of sixteenth century construction although sections of the interior may date from medieval times.

In 1884 it was restored by Lord Stanley of Alderley, whose work showed the influence of his recent conversion to Islam. Much of this was destroyed by fire in 1985, but recent renovation has allowed it to be open to the public once more.

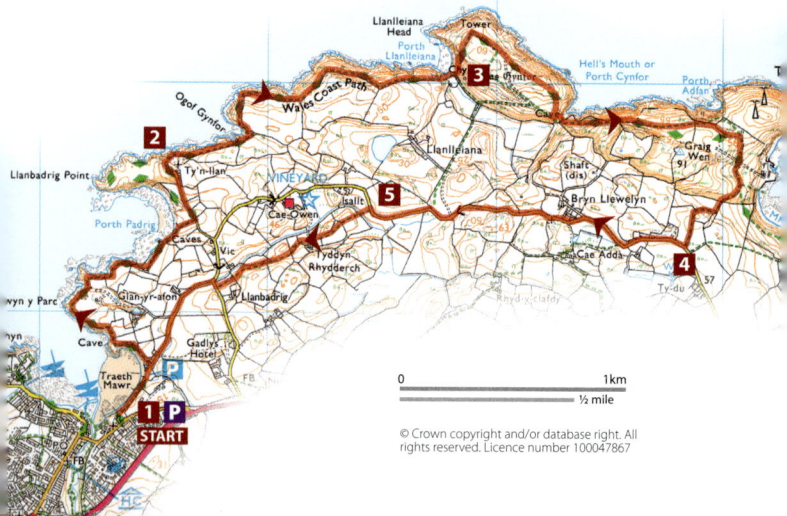

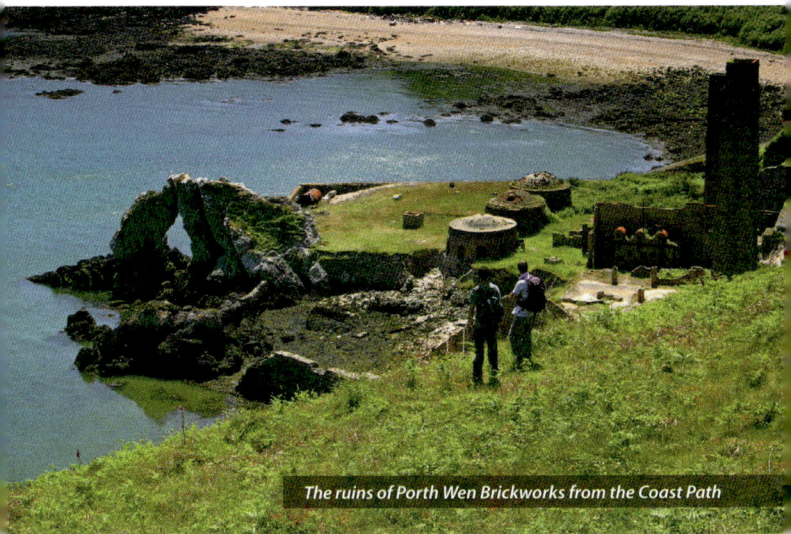

The ruins of Porth Wen Brickworks from the Coast Path

2. Beyond the church, the route heads eastwards and the walk becomes considerably more rugged. Bear left through a **kissing gate** by the church gate and at the **end of the wall** turn right onto the cliff path overlooking the sea. Follow this until you are forced left beside a wire fence with fields ahead.

Go through a kissing gate and keep close by the **fenced fields** on your right as you are very close to **large cliffs** on the left here. After **steps** the path curves right-wards, keeping close to the fields on the right beside the **wall**.

After more **steps** and **two kissing gates** the path continues beside the wall on the right. A little further on a descent is made to the little shingle cove at **Porth Llanlleiana** where there are the ruins of an **old porcelain works**.

In addition to the crumbling buildings there are traces of a small port used to export locally dug china clay.

3. Behind the ruins, a footpath strikes out diagonally to the left up the steep hillside. Once you are up the steep section an easy stroll through heather and bracken take you to the old

The little church of Llanbadrig sits on the very edge of the cliffs

lookout on **Dinas Gynfor** — the most northerly headland on Anglesey.

From here you can see almost the entire northern coast, from Point Lynas in the east to The Skerries off Carmel Head. Between lies some of the wildest and most unspoilt coastline on the island.

From the lookout, an easy path leads through the heather before dropping steeply to **Porth Cynfor**. Ahead, steps lead steeply back to cliff-top level and the angle eases once more. Continue to the wide, rocky bay of Porth Wen.

The old winding gear and the ruined chimneys and kilns below the path are from the long-abandoned Porth Wen Brickworks.

The path curves right above the brickworks and the wide, rocky bay of **Porth Wen** to eventually reach a quiet **lane**.

4. Turn right along the lane for almost 1.5 kilometres/1 mile passing the large house, **Llanlliana** on the right.

5. After a bend, a sign and stile indicate a field path on the left. Turn left here and cut through the centre of a small field to cross a **footbridge**, then aim to the right of a **house** (directly ahead) where gates lead across the access track and into fields once more. Walk ahead

and rise slightly to a gate, then bear right to follow a well defined footpath ahead beside a wire fence and below a **bracken-covered bank**. The path continues through an area of **scrub woodland** to reach a **lane**. Turn right along the lane, then, after about 30 metres turn left and return along the lane to Cemaes Bay to complete the walk. ♦

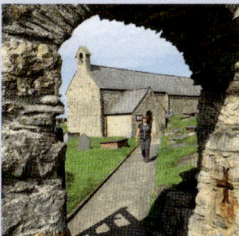

Llanbadrig

This tiny church is dedicated to Saint Patrick, who was sent to convert the Irish by Pope Celestine in the fifth century and reputedly stands on one of the oldest Christian sites in Wales, possibly dating from as early as AD 440. Local legend maintains that Patrick founded the church here in gratitude for his safe arrival ashore, after suffering shipwreck on nearby Ynys Badrig, the small island that can bee seen nearby.

The rocky finger of Point Lynas and its lighthouse

Point Lynas

An impressive section of coast path around Anglesey's northeast tip with wide views along the coast and inland

What to expect:
Good coastal path for much of the time. Some farmland paths and occasional lanes

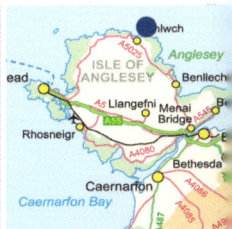

Distance/time: 6 kilometres / 4 miles. Allow 2 hours

Start: Public car park, at Porth Llaneilian, east of Amlwch

Grid ref: SH 475 929

Ordnance Survey Map: Explorer 263 Anglesey East: *Beaumaris, Amlwch & Menai Bridge*

After the walk: 'The Adelphi' or 'Liverpool Arms', Port Amlwch

Walk outline

From the little cove of Porth Eilian, the walk first heads out to Point Lynas where its lighthouse has guided shipping for almost two centuries. The headland is open heath and moorland and a footpath weaves around the lighthouse to a viewpoint . The coast path is then followed along a quiet section of the east coast, before heading inland. The return is made via quiet lanes and farmland paths .

Point Lynas

This long rocky finger marks the northeast tip of Anglesey. It reaches out menacingly into the Liverpool shipping lane and has thus been the site of a lighthouse for almost two centuries.

Point Lynas' unique location, at the junction of two tidal flows along the island's north and east coasts, makes it an important location for whale and dolphin watching, so keep your eyes open. You are most likely to see harbour porpoise, although bottlenose dolphins — around four times the size of a porpoise — are also common. On rare occasions both minke whales and even orcas (killer whales) have been spotted.

Point Lynas Lighthouse

Bottlenose dolphins

The Walk

1. Turn right out of the **car park** and walk down the road towards **Porth Eilian**. At the turning area, bear right following the lane out towards Point Lynas.

2. Before you reach the lighthouse there is a **house** on the right. Go right through a **kissing gate** just after this and follow the footpath that runs parallel with the road. This path will take you around the **lighthouse complex** and out to **Point Lynas** itself.

There has been a beacon at Point Lynas since 1779, although the current lighthouse dates from 1835, and was built by the Mersey Docks and Harbour Board to provide safe passage to vessels travelling to and from Liverpool Docks. The lighthouse is unusual in having the lantern at ground level with the look-out and telegraph room above — much like the Great Orme lighthouse. The semi-circular lantern is located at the base, and operated by Trinity House, whilst the associated keeper's cottages are now popular self-catering holiday homes.

3. Head back to the lighthouse, but keep to the right of the complex and rejoin the

Looking north to Point Lynas and its lighthouse

road just before the house seen earlier. Walk back down the road, through the **stone pillars** and in about 100 metres or so, turn left through a kissing gate, signed for the **coast path**. The path takes you across fields to a second kissing gate, before swinging right along the coast.

4. The coast path crosses two fields above the rocky inlet of **Porth y Corgwl**, then swings left up through an area of scrub (ignore a kissing gate up to the right here) high above **Fresh Water Bay**. After two **footbridges and boadwalks** the path rises to edge rough grazing fields.

As you approach the isolated shingle cove of Porthgwichiaid, you'll see the small island of Ynys Dulas with its cylindrical tower and cone-shaped top. This was built in 1821 by James Hughes of nearby Llys Dulas Manor to store food and provide shelter for shipwrecked seamen.

5. Before the path descends to **Porthygwichiaid**, there is a **ruined brick lookout** building in the field over to the right and a **small wooden estate information board** beside the footpath.

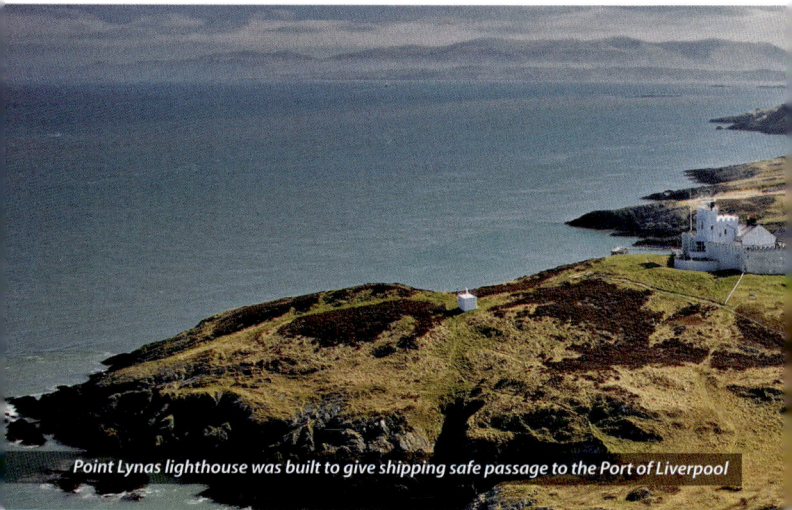

Point Lynas lighthouse was built to give shipping safe passage to the Port of Liverpool

There is a faint footpath on the right here that heads inland. Take this path through low gorse to eventually reach a stile beside a gate leading into a narrow **tarmac lane**.

Turn right along the lane and in around 500-metres look for a signed path on the right. This heads along an access road and is signed for **The Old Telegraph**.

The Old Telegraph was built in 1841 by the Trustees of the Liverpool Docks and is one of a dozen signal stations built along the North Wales coast from Liverpool to Holyhead. From 1860 onwards the semaphore system was gradually replaced by electrical transmission and the 12 stations were reduced to five. This station was eventually made redundant and a signal staff then installed at Point Lynas lighthouse. The Old Telegraph station is now a private residence.

Turn right and follow the access road past a junction of footpaths and on to a large metal gate — the entrance to **Refail Hir**. Immediately before the gate, bear right onto a signed footpath.

6. This path leads downhill between high hedgerows. Ignore a left into 'Coed Avens', keeping ahead to eventually reach a **tarmac lane** opposite houses.

Turn right over a **cattle grid** and cross a stile almost immediately on the left. The right of way follows the left-hand field edge, crosses a stile in the lower corner, then keeps to the right-hand field edges, before finally cutting through an area of bracken and gorse on the right to reach a **lane**.

Turn left and follow the lane above Porth Eilian back to the car park to complete the walk. ♦

Whale and dolphin watch

Point Lynas is a great place for spotting cetaceans — one of the top locations in the UK, in fact. Located at the junction of tides merging from the north and east coasts of the island, it concentrates the small fish on which marine mammals feed. It was here that the largest group of Risso's dolphins — around fifty individuals — was sighted in 2015. There is also a good chance of seeing bottlenose dolphins, minke whales and even — on very rare occasions — killer whales.

On the Coast Path near Traeth yr Ora

Traeth Lligwy

Straightforward walking on good paths along the coast and through farmland. A return along quiet lanes

What to expect:

Good coastal path followed by farmland footpaths and quiet lanes

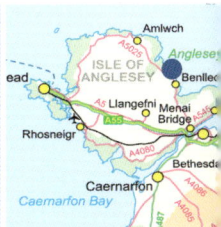

Distance/time: 6.5 kilometres / 4½ miles. Allow 2½-3 hours

Start: Begin the walk at the beach car park, Traeth Lligwy.

Grid ref: SH 497 871

Ordnance Survey Map: Explorer 263 Anglesey East: *Beaumaris, Amlwch & Menai Bridge*

After the walk: Pub on the route at Brynrefail, pub and café in nearby Moelfre, summer beach café at Traeth Lligwy

Walk outline

A straightforward walk along the coastal path from Traeth Lligwy visiting the quiet cove of Traeth yr Ora and the tidal estuary of Traeth Dulas. This is followed by easy footpaths through farmland, with the option to call in for a mid-walk drink and snack at the Pilot Boat Inn. Return is along quiet lanes.

Traeth Lligwy and Traeth Dulas

Traeth Lligwy is one of the best beaches on the eastern side of Anglesey — a wide sandy bay in a sheltered location, backed by farmland and scattered woods. Two large beach car parks and easy access attract the crowds on fine days, but an easy jaunt along the Coast Path to the secluded cove of Traeth yr Ora and the broad, but largely unknown tidal estuary of Traeth Dulas, is ideal for those seeking peace and quiet.

Traeth Dulas is a superb location for birdwatching. Invertebrates in the open mud and sand provide rich pickings for all sorts of waders, from redshanks to curlews. Little egrets are an increasingly common sight around Welsh tidal estuaries too, their white plumage making them easy to spot.

Dulas estuary wreck

Little egrets

The Walk

1. Walk through the car park away from the little beach bar/café (with the beach to your right). Cut through the dunes and cross a **wooden footbridge** and smaller **stone bridge** to reach a second car park. The coast path exits the car park at the far end.

The path is straightforward now above the beach, following a series of low scrub-covered rocks and passing a ruined brick lookout tower. The first cove is **Porth y Môr**, a small shingle beach. The path drops down briefly onto the shingle, before continuing to **Traeth yr Ora**.

2. Above Traeth yr Ora there is a three-way path junction and a bench seat. The coast path turns left here, but it is well worth the short circuit of **Glastir**, a small headland with an open access agreement. For this option go ahead and return to this junction to continue.

Returning to the junction above Traeth yr Ora, turn right (left if you didn't bother with Glastir) and follow the path up to **Penrhyn farm**. Turn right at the farm along an access

track and bear right at a **caravan site access road**. At a tarmac road a little further on, turn right to go through a kissing gate into a field. Walk ahead up the field through a second kissing gate and keep ahead up a larger field keeping close to the left-hand fence. At the end of the fence turn left and follow a section of fenced path.

3. At the end of the fenced section, walk ahead through the following field passing a **large pool**. Go through a kissing gate and along a farm track. Where this bears right, go through the kissing gate ahead and across the field to reach a lane by the **Pilot Boat Inn**.

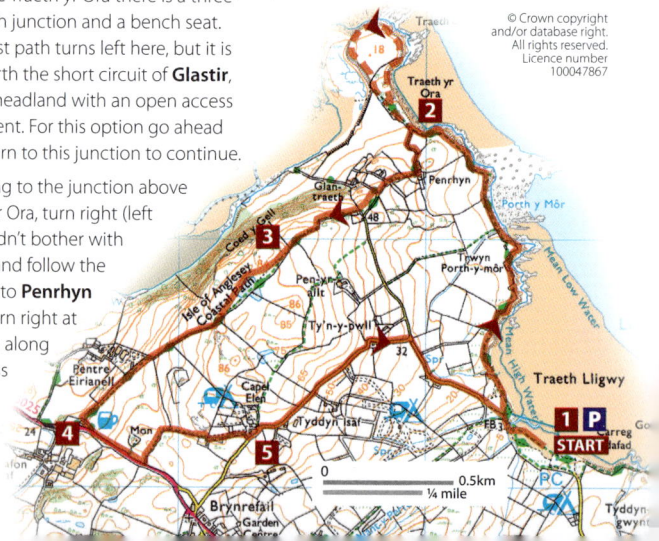

The footpath connecting the two beach car parks

4. Turn left alongside the road and in around 250 metres you will see a signed path to the **Morris Brothers Memorial** (see the box below). About 100 metres further on, take the signed path also on the left. This path keeps to the field edge passing through a kissing gate. In the top corner cross a ladder stile into a **caravan site**. Turn left along the site road briefly and where this swings left, keep ahead on a broad grass path with caravans on the left.

5. At the lane turn left. At the T-junction turn right and follow the lane back to the car park. Cross the two footbridges to complete the walk. ♦

Morris Memorial

The four Morris brothers grew up at Pentre Eirianell just below the 'Pilot Boat Inn' in the early eighteenth century. They became famous for the many thousands of letters they wrote to each other during their working lives which have remarkably survived and give a fascinating glimpse of life in rural Wales, particularly Anglesey, during that period. Lewis Morris, the eldest of the brothers, is also noted for his sea charts, which were published in 1784.

Seawatch Centre and Lifeboat Station, Moelfre

Moelfre

An easy walk on an attractive section of coast centered on the village resort of Moelfre

What to expect:
Well marked coast path, field paths and country lanes

Distance/time: 7.25 kilometres / 4½ miles. Allow 2 hours

Start: Begin the walk at the beach car park, Traeth Lligwy.

Grid ref: SH 497 871

Ordnance Survey Map: Explorer 263 Anglesey East: *Beaumaris, Amlwch & Menai Bridge*

After the walk: Pub and café on the route in Moelfre, seasonal beach café at Traeth Lligwy

Walk outline

From Traeth Lligwy a straightforward coast path leads along the low limestone cliffs to the village of Moelfre. Beach cafés, a handful of shops and a pub allow for a mid walk break before the route heads inland along lanes. There are some fascinating relics from the island's prehistory to see here: the Lligwy Burial Chamber, an amazing neolithic burial chamber and Din Ligwy, a fourth-century British settlement. Return is by quiet lanes.

Moelfre

Moelfre is one the most attractive coastal villages on the island. The tiny sea front and pebble beach is south facing and protected by a headland to the north. The prevailing westerlies, even on a blustery day, have largely exhausted themselves by the time they reach this part of the island and visitors can often enjoy warm early spring or late autumn sunshine here.

Points of interest include the Seawatch Centre and nearby Ynys Moelfre with its large colonies of breeding sea birds, notably cormorants and shags, and the historic sites of Din Lligwy, Hen Capel and Lligwy Burial Chamber.

'Royal Charter' *memorial*

Cormorant

The Walk

1. From the car park turn right (when looking out to sea) along the coastal path. This is well defined with a view across **Traeth Lligwy** with **Ynys Dulas** and its curious tower beyond. The first cove — **Porth Forllwyd** — is private and the path takes a right turn across a small field to join an access road. Turn left, pass a cottage ('Moryn') on the left and at the end of the **wall** the path rejoins the coast to run along a series of low limestone cliffs.

On the approach to the small shingle inlet of Porth Helaeth, you will see a stone memorial commemorating the wreck, in 1859, of the Royal Charter:

In its day, the Royal Charter *was one of the fastest clippers on the run between Liverpool and Australia and could make the journey in under 60 days. On August 26th 1859, she left Melbourne laden with passengers who had made their fortune in the Australian goldfields. Eight weeks later she was almost within sight of Liverpool after a journey of 16,000 miles when one of the worst storms of the century drove her onto rocks little more than a stone's throw from here. There were survivors, but very few; 465 lives were lost. The whole country was shocked by the disaster.*

2. From the cove, the footpath rises to a **caravan site** then bears left along the coast to open land on a small headland.

The neolithic Lligwy Burial Chamber with its massive capstone

Keep to the signed coast path ignoring paths on the right until you reach the narrow channel of **Y Swnt** with **Ynys Moelfre** ahead. Cross a small shingle beach by cottages and at the far end turn right on a tarmac footpath past the **lifeboat station** and **Seawatch Centre**.

Beyond the Seawatch Centre, the path bears right to **Moelfre harbour**. Join the road here and turn left along the front, then up the hill passing the **Kinmel Arms** on the right and the **anchor** taken from the wreck of the *Hindlea*, lost on October 27th 1959 almost 100 years to

the day after the loss of the *Royal Charter* and in almost the same location.

3. Take the first road on the right and continue for 1 kilometre/ ¾ mile.

Immediately after the entrance to **quarry workings** on the left, turn left through a kissing gate onto a signed path. Rise to a second kissing gate and follow the right of way ahead along field edges. In the far corner of the second field, turn right over a stone stile and along the field edge to a quiet lane.

4. Turn left here and follow the lane for about 300 metres to visit the **Lligwy**

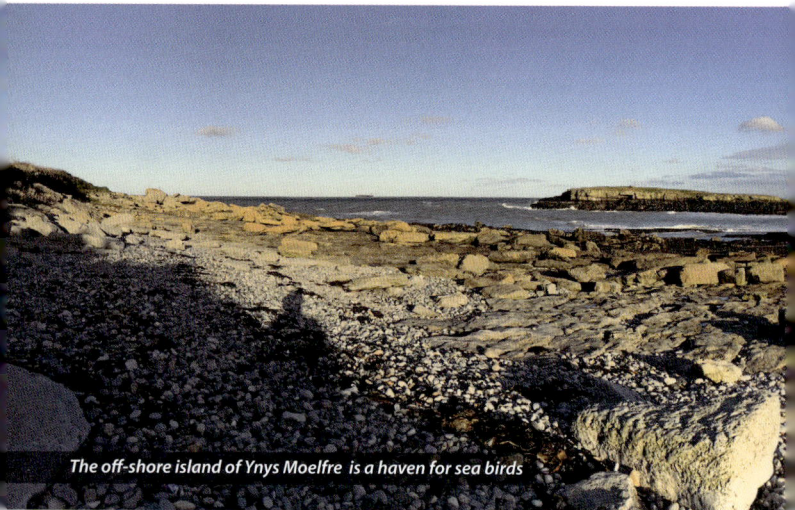

The off-shore island of Ynys Moelfre is a haven for sea birds

Burial Chamber, which lies in fields to the right.

The most obvious feature of this neolithic burial chamber (Circa 2,500BC) is the massive capstone: over 18 feet long and nearly 16 feet wide. It is estimated to weigh some 25 tons and was probably lifted into place with the aid of timber scaffolding. Two thirds of the chamber lie below ground level and make use of a natural fissure in the rock giving the chamber a very squat appearance. The entrance faces east towards the lane and originally the whole structure would have been covered by a mound of earth and stones which has been eroded away.

Retrace your steps along the road passing the spot where you entered the lane. Beyond this, look for the signed footpath to **Din Lligwy** and **Hen Capel** on the left.

5. The path keeps beside the fence on your left with the ruins of Hen Capel to your right. A metal kissing gate takes you into a small wood where a short rise leads to Din Lligwy (see box opposite).

Retrace your steps to the lane passing Hen Capel, standing alone and isolated in the fields overlooking the bay.

Hen Capel or 'Old Chapel' dates from the twelfth century when most early Celtic

churches were built in stone for the first time. By this period, Anglesey was free from the fear of Viking raids and the lower parts of the walls survive from this time. Inside, the walls were originally rendered.

Turn left along the lane and at the crossroads go straight ahead returning to the beach car park to complete the walk. ♦

Din Lligwy

Din Lligwy is one of the most remarkable and best preserved British settlements in the country and is thought to date from the middle of the fourth century, a period when the Romans were withdrawing from North Wales. It is thought to have been the dwelling of a local chieftain or ruler and consists of a total of nine buildings; seven rectangular and two circular, which would originally have been thatched.

Useful Information

Wales Coast Path

Comprehensive information about all sections of the **Wales Coast Path** can be found at: **www.walescoastpath.co.uk** and **www.walescoastpath.gov.uk**

Visit Wales

The Visit Wales website covers everything from accommodation and events to attractions and adventure. For information on the area covered by this book, see: **www.visitwales.co.uk**

Isle of Anglesey/ Ynys Môn Tourist Information

Discover more about the Isle of Anglesey and its coast, from where to stay, what to do, events and food and drink. See: **www.anglesey.gov.uk** or **www.visitanglesey.co.uk**

Tourist Information Centres

There are no longer any TICs on the Isle of Anglesey.

Travel

Public Transport for services in all parts of Wales are available from Traveline Cymru. Call 0871 200 22 33 or see: **www.traveline-cymru.info**

Tide Times

Some walks depend on tide times, and it's important to check before starting out. For details see **www.tidetimes.org.uk** and calculate the tide times according to location. You can also pick up copies of traditional printed tide tables from local shops for around £1.

Weather

The Met Office operates a 24 hour online weather forecast. See www.metoffice.gov.uk